Aaron J

The Inspirational Story of Football Superstar Aaron Rodgers

Copyright 2015 by Bill Redban - All rights reserved.

This document is geared towards providing exact and reliable information in regards to the topic and issue covered. The publication is sold with the idea that the publisher is not required to render accounting, officially permitted, or otherwise, qualified services. If advice is necessary, legal or professional, a practiced individual in the profession should be ordered.

In no way is it legal to reproduce, duplicate, or transmit any part of this document in either electronic means or in printed format. Recording of this publication is strictly prohibited and any storage of this document is not allowed unless with written permission from the publisher. All rights reserved.

The information provided herein is stated to be truthful and consistent, in that any liability, in terms of inattention or otherwise, by any usage or abuse of any policies, processes, or directions contained within is the solitary and utter responsibility of the recipient reader. Under no circumstances will any legal responsibility or blame be held against the publisher for any reparation, damages, or monetary loss due to the information herein, either directly or indirectly.

The information herein is offered for informational purposes solely, and is universal as so. The presentation of the information is without contract or any type of guarantee assurance.

The trademarks that are used are without any consent, and the publication of the trademark is without permission or backing by the trademark owner. All trademarks and brands within this book are for clarifying purposes only and are the owned by the owners themselves, not affiliated with this document.

Table Of Contents

Introduction

Chapter 1: Early Childhood and Youth

Chapter 2: School Career

Chapter 3: Professional Life

Chapter 4: Personal Adult Life

Chapter 5: Philanthropies and Charitable Acts

Chapter 6: Notable Statistics and Career Milestones

Conclusion

Introduction

As the title already implies, this is a book about [The Inspirational Story of Football Superstar Aaron Rodgers] and how he rose from his life in the Chico, California area to becoming one of today's leading and most-respected football players. In his rise to superstardom, Aaron has inspired not only the youth, but fans of all ages, throughout the world.

This book also portrays the struggles that Aaron has had to overcome during his early childhood years, his teen years, and up until he became what he is today. A notable source of inspiration is Rodger's own Foundation that was named after him, as well as his consistent support of other charitable organizations such as the Boys and Girls Foundation, as well as numerous others. He continues to serve as the jovial superstar who loves to play the underdog role and prove doubters wrong every Sunday.

Combining incredible accuracy, sharp decision making, quick feet, and superior coordination, Aaron has shown the ability to slice up just about any kind of defense. From being an overlooked high school kid that nobody wanted to give a scholarship to, to being one of the greatest quarterbacks of his generation, you'll learn here how this man has risen to the ranks of the best football players today.

Thanks again for downloading this book. Hopefully you can take some lessons from Aaron's life and apply them to your own!

Chapter 1:

Early Childhood and Youth

It may be wise to say that Aaron Charles Rodgers was infused with a football DNA. He was born on December 2nd, 1983 in Chico, California to Darla Leigh Pittman Rodgers and Edward Wesley Rodgers. His football genes came from his dad, who was a former offensive lineman for California State University, Chico and ended up becoming a chiropractor. Aaron's football inclination was seen early on, as he started watching National Football League games at the age of two. By the age of five, Aaron was already collecting football cards and trying to memorize the statistics of each of his favorite players.

As part of their bonding sessions, Edward would throw the pigskin around with his sons, Jordan,

Luke, and Aaron. While they were playing catch, Edward would impart in them wisdom that went beyond football. At an early age, their father told the boys not to take alcoholic drinks and avoid late-night parties when they got to college, for it could diminish their talents on the field.

Aaron took this advice seriously and would carry it with him throughout his high school and college years. He became an example of success through hard work, even at a young age. Aaron's focus and drive led him not only to football success, but success in other sports as well, such as basketball and baseball.

Aaron spent his early childhood years between Ukiah, California and Beaverton, Oregon, where he attended Oak Manor Elementary School, Vose Elementary School and Whitford Middle School, respectively. Even though he changed schools often, Aaron still continued to develop his athletic abilities no matter where he was at. At the age of 10, Aaron received positive attention after a local newspaper in Ukiah reported his impressive performance at a free throw shooting contest. While he was in Oregon, young Aaron showed his baseball skills by playing in the Raleigh Hills Little League and shuffled between the positions of pitcher, shortstop and centerfielder.

Due to his preference for baseball and football, Aaron followed the games of the Los Angeles Dodgers and the San Francisco 49ers. However, he started to follow football even more closely when quarterback Joe Montana became his ultimate sports idol. Aaron's youth was a perfect time to grow up as a fan of the Bay Area team, because the 49ers were perennial championship contenders, thanks to their gritty defense and vaunted West Coast offense.

In 1997, Aaron's family moved back to Chico, California where Aaron would spend most of his adolescent years. It was also during this time that the young Aaron Rodgers would decide to focus on football rather than baseball.

After moving back to Chico, Aaron enrolled at Pleasant Valley High School with two goals in mind: to become a commendable student and to be the top quarterback of the school's varsity football team. He was a great student all throughout high school but would attain his latter goal during his junior season, when he was finally given the reins of the football team.

As a third year student, Aaron threw for over 2,000 passing yards and was named to the All-Section team. As an encore, he amassed 2,303 passing yards in his senior season, which is a record that still stands. He also set other records, such as the most touchdown passes in a single game, with six, as well as the most all-purpose yards in a single contest, with 440 yards. At the end of the season, Aaron was once again included on the All-Section squad.

Away from the gridiron, Rodgers achieved high grades in his classes. His hard work in his classes made him eligible for either an academic or athletic scholarship. However, football was where his heart was and it was what he wanted to pursue after high school, even though he had a high Scholastic Assessment Test (SAT) score, which was estimated to be in the 1300-1400 range.

Despite all of his individual accolades at Pleasant Valley, NCAA Division I colleges were not interested in Rodgers, one of the possible factors being that he was on a losing team. Also, college recruiters were not high on his physical attributes, especially his height, because he was barely six feet. With the defensive players in college being bigger and stronger, the theory that many scouts believed was that a taller quarterback would be necessary in order to see over the line. (Scouts have now become less rigid with this, due to the success of quarterbacks such as Drew Brees, Russell Wilson, and Johnny Manziel, to name a few.)

Despite the lack of college recruiting attention, Aaron kept his desire to play football at the next level in tact. He preferred to play under the legendary coach, Bobby Bowden, at Florida State University. However, Aaron's scholarship application was rejected. He would soon get an invitation from the University of Illinois as a walk-on, but he eventually declined because there was no assurance of him making the roster. These setbacks initially pushed him to consider applying for an academic scholarship and eventually take up law.

However, after much consideration, Aaron never gave up on what he really wanted and continued his pursuit of football. With no Division I school willing to give him a shot, he accepted the offer to play as the quarterback of Butte Community College. This scenario gave him a chance to continue playing the sport that he loved while still staying close to home, because Butte was just around 15 miles southeast of Chico.

Chapter 2:

School Career

To no surprise, Aaron blossomed under the guidance of Coach Craig Rigsbee at Butte Community College. He was named starting quarterback of the team even though he was a freshman, but he did not disappoint. Aaron led the Roadrunners to a 10-1 record and a No. 2 NCAA national junior college ranking, thanks to his 28 touchdown passes. At the end of the year, his team also clinched the championship of the NorCal conference. Aside from his impressive stats and accomplishments, Aaron added some height and bulk to become the prototypical NCAA Division I quarterback.

However, Aaron was not the most touted athlete on the team among college scouts. Rather, it was tight end Garrett Cross, who was being recruited by the University of California, Berkeley. But as fate would have it, UCBerkeley head coach, Jeff Tedford, who was originally watching Cross through game tapes, also noticed that Rodgers threw for six touchdown passes in one game. This performance spiked Tedford's interest in Rodgers as well, and he informed Rigsbee of his attendance at Butte's next practice.

With an opportunity to play NCAA Division I on the line, Rigsbee altered the course of the practice a bit. From the usual walk-throughs, Rigsbee devised a few passing drills for Rodgers, so that Tedford could have an ample assessment of the quarterback's skills. Tedford was so impressed by Rodgers' form and arm strength that he offered the kid from Chico a football scholarship, as he was driving back home to Berkeley. Rodgers accepted the offer and he was able to immediately transfer to Cal Berkeley by virtue of his high SAT score. Normally, players from junior colleges could only transfer to a Division I program after playing two years.

Since Rodgers was a junior college transferee, he only had three years of eligibility left at Cal. In his first season with the Golden Bears, Aaron played sparingly during the first four games. However, the team's coaching staff took notice of his superb in-game decision making, and Aaron was named the starting quarterback for the team's fifth game. Ironically, Aaron would be facing the only university that gave him an offer: Illinois.

His second start proved to be an even bigger challenge as the Golden Bears went up against the Trojans of the University of Southern California, which was a consistent Division I football powerhouse. But through Aaron's efforts, Cal Berkeley was able to pull off an upset over USC in triple overtime. Some college scouts were scratching their heads over Rodgers' meteoric rise and he would go on to post a 6-3 win-loss record as a starter, while having a streak of 98 completions without an interception. His completion percentage, at the time, was also an impressive 68.2 percent.

Before the University of California, Berkeley Golden Bears made it to the Insight Bowl to play against Virginia Tech, Rodgers would record memorable performances in must-win games, against Washington and Stanford, respectively. In the battle against the Cardinal, Rodgers threw for 414 yards. Hardened by these tough games, Aaron would give his alma mater a post-

Christmas gift in the form of an Insight Bowl victory, wherein he threw for 394 yards.

At the end of the season, Aaron would collect 2,903 passing yards and 19 passing touchdowns with only five interceptions. What made this even more impressive was the fact that Aaron spent his first few games as a back-up quarterback. He would go on to tie a school record, with five 300-yard passing games, and set a new benchmark for the lowest intercepted pass percentage of 1.43%.

With a growing reputation, Aaron proved that his first season at Cal Berkeley was no fluke, as he led a highly-potent passing attack, in his second season, that averaged 37 points per game. Aside from his pin-point accuracy, the Golden Bears' ground game was also in full-stride (no pun intended), as it averaged nearly 270 yards per game. In the middle of it all, Aaron collected 2,566 passing yards with 24 touchdowns and a passer rating that was runner-up to only USC's Matt Leinart.

The Golden Bears would go on to lose to USC in the regular season by a touchdown, but their 10-1 record was enough to win the Pac 10

Conference championship. Normally, a record like this would be worthy of a Rose Bowl invitation. However, the University of Texas Longhorns were named on their behalf and the Golden Bears were slated against Texas Tech University in the Holiday Bowl. Texas Tech would win and this eventually became Rodgers' last game in college, as he would declare for the 2005 N.F.L. Draft.

During his first year with the Golden Bears, Rodgers was an All-Pac 10 Honorable Mention and Insight Bowl Most Valuable Player in 2003. The following year, he was named Cal Co-Offensive MVP, First Team Pac-10, Second Team Academic All Pac-10 and an Honorable Mention All-American by Sports Illustrated.

Not bad for a player that no major football programs really wanted.

Chapter 3:

Professional Life

Coming into the 2005 N.F.L. Draft, Rodgers was projected as the number two quarterback prospect behind Alex Smith of Utah. However, some experts predicted that Rodgers would have a better career than Smith. Despite the speculations, Rodgers wanted to be the number one overall draft choice, not only because of the prestige that came with it, but mainly due to the fact that the team with the first pick was his hometown team, the San Francisco 49ers. If the 49ers decided to pick him, he would be fulfilling a dream that he had been nurturing ever since his early childhood.

However, San Francisco chose Smith based on some factors they wanted in a quarterback. One of the things that N.F.L. scouts often pointed out, was that Rodgers played in a quarterback-friendly system that might not work against the complex defensive strategies in the professional football circuit. The majority of the teams held it against him and this led to Rodgers' terrible draft day experience.

Rodgers was invited to the N.F.L. Draft's green room, wherein family, friends, and agents can join the prospect until his name is called. Usually, the green room prospects are drafted early on. However, Rodgers had to wait a long time, as twenty-three other names were called before his. Eventually, he was picked by the Green Bay Packers. This would guarantee him a rookie contract, but playing time was another issue, because the team had one of the top N.F.L. passers of all-time, in Brett Favre.

Before the inclusion of Rodgers to the Packers, the team won its third consecutive division title and quarterback was one of the positions that they had covered. Still, the team signed Rodgers to a five-year, $7.7 million deal with $5.4 million guaranteed. Aaron was involved in the offensive sequences of the team during the offseason and he was mainly used to mimic opposing quarterbacks during team practices. On a bad play of fortune though, injuries would take a toll on the Packers, as they limped through a 4-12 season. Rodgers appeared in only three official games during his rookie season, gaining 65 yards on nine completed passes.

Aaron's second and third seasons with the Packers were no different. In two seasons, he would play four games and register 26 completions for 264 yards and 9 rushing attempts for 40 yards. However, Coach Mike McCarthy took over for Mike Sherman and he conducted special training for Rodgers. These sessions helped to improve all of the intangibles that the young quarterback would need to become an N.F.L. starter. Now, Aaron was ready for the limelight. Yet, it seemed that Brett Favre would stay with the Packers for a while, or at least as long as he wanted to.

In March of 2008, Brett Favre announced his retirement from the N.F.L, which meant the starting quarterback position was Rodgers' to lose. However, Favre sparked drama within the Packers organization when he decided to come back and play another season. Eventually, Green Bay's starting quarterback for 16 seasons was traded to the New York Jets and Rodgers was named the starter for the 2008 season.

His sessions with Coach Mike McCarthy would pay off, as Aaron registered a sensational first season as a starter. By the end of the season, Aaron gained over 4,000 passing yards with 28 touchdowns and only 13 interceptions. However, his inexperience eventually showed as the Packers lost seven games decided by a touchdown or less. Still, his impressive form left no reason for the Packers not to give him a generous contract extension, worth $65 million for six years.

The new contract proved to be a motivating factor for Rodgers to improve on his second season as the team's starter. During that year, Aaron won his first come-from-behind game against the Chicago Bears, and he was named the NFC Offensive Player of the Month for October. The team played well during the second half of the season and the Packers posted an 11-5 regular season record as well as a playoff berth. However, the Packers lost in the playoffs to the Arizona Cardinals, in the highest scoring playoff game in N.F.L. history, 51-45. Rodgers amassed another 4,000 passing yard season and the single season total was just behind Lynn Dickey's all-time Packers single-season passing record.

For the 2010 season, Rodgers wanted to avenge the bitter loss against the Cardinals, which ended in a sack and a fumble recovery for the walk-in touchdown. The team won its first two games but lost the next three of four. To make matters worse, Rodgers suffered a concussion and Matt Flynn took his place during the games when Aaron was injured. The team finished the regular season at 10-6 but their defeats were by a margin of four points or less.

As the Wild Card sixth seed, the Packers defeated the Philadelphia Eagles in the Wild Card round and the Atlanta Falcons in the Divisional round. They would become NFC Champions by defeating the Chicago Bears and eventually, Super Bowl champions by defeating the Pittsburgh Steelers. Rodgers would be named the Super Bowl MVP, a distinction that Brett Favre did not win in his distinguished career.

With a championship in tow, it seemed that Aaron Rodgers and the Packers were poised for another championship season in 2011. They started the regular season with 13 straight wins and eventually ended at 15-1, with the sole loss coming to the Kansas City Chiefs in Week 15. However, they lost in the first round of the playoffs to the New York Giants and another great season went down the drain. During the regular season, Rodgers had one of the finest seasons any quarterback could have by passing for 4,643 yards with 45 touchdowns and just six interceptions.

The 2012 season would provide a rough start for the Packers, with the team splitting their first four games. Add to that, the "Fail Mary" game against the Seattle Seahawks, where a controversial call went against the Packers in the final seconds of the game. Still, the Packers finished with an 11-5 record but eventually bowed out of the postseason in the divisional round against the San Francisco 49ers. By the end of the season, Aaron compiled 4,295 yards and 39 touchdown passes.

By 2013, Aaron was once again rewarded with a five-year, $110 million contract and had a strong start to the season. However, a sack by Shea McClellin caused Rodgers' clavicle to break and he is expected to miss a month because of it. As of his last game with the Packers, Aaron has compiled career statistics of 22,718 passing yards, 179 passing touchdowns, 1,833 completions and only 49 interceptions.

Chapter 4:

Personal Adult Life

Aaron is a devout Catholic but he is not known to express his faith publicly, like players such as Tim Tebow or Ray Lewis. He lives by St. Francis of Assissi's creed of "Preach the gospel at all times. If necessary, use words."

One thing that Brett Favre and Aaron Rodgers have in common is their jolly demeanor. Not surprisingly, Rodgers is regarded as one of the best photo bombers in the National Football League. He usually photo bombs the pictures of team captains during the coin toss.

After a rushing touchdown, Rodgers likes to perform his "championship belt" gesture by placing his hands around his waist area and pulling them apart, as if he just put on a title belt. This move was parlayed into an endorsement deal with State Farm Insurance. In a string of commercials, the "Discount Double Check" move that the advertising actors perform, is the same as Rodgers' championship belt gesture. Aside from that, he has also appeared on a Wheaties box and has other endorsements with Nike and Pizza Hut.

Many players around the league say that Aaron plays with a chip on his shoulder, as if he has something to prove. He also has admitted that he loves playing in the underdog role because he loves to prove doubters wrong. He was doubted at pretty much every stage of his career; when coming out of high school, coming out of college, as well as having to wait patiently for Brett Favre to finally make a decision before he could prove himself worthy as a starter in the N.F.L.

Rodgers is also known to have a relationship with Milwaukee Brewers baseball star, Ryan Braun. They were both co-owners of a restaurant in the Milwaukee area. However, after the Ryan Braun PED scandal, they went separate ways as far as business partners.

On a family note, Aaron's younger brother, Jordan, played quarterback for Vanderbilt University, and briefly played for the Jacksonville Jaguars, as well. Recently, Aaron was engaged to fellow Chico native, Destiny Newton. He currently lives in Del Mar, California, which is about 20 miles north of San Diego. Aaron also has a home in Suamico, Wisconsin.

Chapter 5:

Philanthropies and Charitable Acts

Aaron is one of the most charitable players in all of the National Football League. Recently, he surprised a fan, living with Spina Bifida, by recording a song and playing the guitar with her. The proceedings of this meet-up are posted on the itsaaron.com website, which was founded by Rodgers and David Gruber. This website aims to make people aware of life-changing circumstances, individuals and organizations.

Also, Aaron has organized a fundraising banquet in Milwaukee, Wisconsin for the Midwest Athletes Against Childhood Cancer fund. He also co-hosted three charity golf events with Young Life Foundation and is a regular participant in the Andy North and Friends Golf Tournament, which raises funds for the Paul P. Carbone Comprehensive Cancer Research Center at the University of Wisconsin.

Rodgers also participates in other charity events, such as the American Century Celebrity Golf Championship, the Edgar Bennett Celebrity Bowl-a-Thon and the Vince Lombardi Golf Classic. In 2010, Aaron participated in the Twelve Days of Christmas charity initiative for the children who were under the care of The Salvation Army and the Ecumenical Partnership for Housing. The kids were given a shopping spree and a party, where they could meet and mingle with other Green Bay Packers players.

Aaron Rodgers' inspirational story is one of motivation and determination. Even though there were moments in his life that did not go well, he kept on pushing himself to achieve his dreams. When he was given an opportunity, he made the most out of it, which ultimately led him to the success that he now enjoys. There were times that he had his back against the ropes, but by having an unbreakable fighting spirit, failure was not an option for him.

Likewise, he became grateful for what he has achieved by sharing his time and his personality to whoever needs it. He has participated in a number of charity initiatives and his appearances are not likely to wane down in the coming years. Being one of the more popular and marketable players in the National Football League, Rodgers uses his star power wisely, by convincing others to lend a helping hand and to provide young people a role model that they can look up to.

Aaron makes it a point to always spread the message of "believing in yourself". This is very important to him because he knows that he was one of the few people in the world that had faith in himself coming out of high school. His message is clear; if a guy can become an MVP caliber player in the National Football League after struggling to get a Division I scholarship offer out of high school, what excuse do you have to not work hard to follow your own dream?

Chapter 6:

Notable Statistics and Career Milestones

Along with Peyton Manning, Tom Brady, and Drew Brees, Aaron Rodgers has been debated as being the best quarterback in the N.F.L. over the last half decade. It is extremely difficult to compare quarterbacks in the current era because of the quarterback-friendly rules, as well as the different abilities that quarterbacks possess these days. Players like Colin Kaepernick and Cam Newton have different effects on the game than someone like Peyton Manning, and vice-versa. However, there is no doubt that statistically, Aaron Rodgers is one of the best quarterbacks to ever play. The statistics don't lie...

Aaron is the only National Football League quarterback to have a career passer rating of over 100 and to have a passer rating of at least 100 for both the regular season and the playoffs.

He also has the highest career passer rating in the regular season with 105.2, on a minimum of 1,500 passing attempts. His postseason career rating of 103.6 is third all-time.

His career pass to interception percentage of 1.7% is the lowest in N.F.L. history. Likewise, he has the best touchdown to interception ratio in the N.F.L. and the second-highest completion percentage in the regular season, with 65.8%.

Aaron also holds the record for most passing yards by a quarterback in his first playoff game, with 423, and the most touchdown passes in his first three playoff games, with ten.

Aaron is also the only quarterback to have collected at least 4,000 passing yards in his first two seasons as a starter and only the sixth quarterback to register at least 1,000 passing yards in a single postseason run.

He also holds the record for the most consecutive games without more than one interception, with 41, and the most consecutive games with at least two touchdown passes, with 13. His 42 interceptions are the fewest by any quarterback before getting their 150th touchdown pass.

Aaron is also the third quarterback in N.F.L. history to throw for 30 touchdown passes in one season, before his 30th birthday. He also holds the record for most consecutive postseason games with at least three touchdowns, with three, and is the only N.F.L. quarterback to have at least 45 touchdown passes and at most, six interceptions, in a single season.

Aaron was named FedEx Air Player of the Week seven times and NFC Player of the Month six times.

Conclusion

I hope this book was able to help you to gain inspiration from the life of Aaron Rodgers, one of the best players currently playing in the National Football League.

The rise and fall of a star is often the cause for much wonder. But most stars have an expiration date. In football, once a star player reaches his mid- to late-thirties, it is often time to contemplate retirement. What will be left in people's minds about that fading star? In Aaron Rodgers' case, people will remember how he led his team in their journey towards a Super Bowl. He will be remembered as the guy who replaced the "un-replaceable", helped the team build their image again, while honing his own image along the way.

Rodgers has also inspired so many people because he is the star who never failed to look back, who paid his dues forward by helping thousands of less-fortunate youth find their inner light through sports and education.

And another thing that stands out in Aaron's history is the fact that he never forgot where he came from. As soon as he had the capacity to give back, he poured what he had straight back to those who needed it, and he continues to do so to this day. Last but not least, he's remarkable for remaining simple and firm with his principles in spite of his immense popularity.

Hopefully you learned some great things about Aaron in this book and are able to apply what you've learned to your own life!

Other Football Stories That Will Inspire You!

Tom Brady

http://www.amazon.com/dp/B00HJYQTRS

Peyton Manning

http://www.amazon.com/dp/B00HJUYTCY

Colin Kaepernick

http://www.amazon.com/dp/B00IRHHABU

Russell Wilson

http://www.amazon.com/dp/B00HK909C8

Calvin Johnson

http://www.amazon.com/dp/B00HJK0YS2

Inspirational Basketball Stories!

Stephen Curry

http://www.amazon.com/dp/B00HH9QU1A

Derrick Rose

http://www.amazon.com/dp/B00HH1BE82

Blake Griffin

http://www.amazon.com/dp/B00INNVVIG

Carmelo Anthony

http://www.amazon.com/dp/B00HH9L3P8

Chris Paul

http://www.amazon.com/dp/B00HIZXMSW

Paul George

http://www.amazon.com/dp/B00IN3YIVI

Dirk Nowitzki

http://www.amazon.com/dp/B00HRVPD9I

Kevin Durant

http://www.amazon.com/dp/B00HIKDK34

Other Inspirational Stories!

Mike Trout

http://www.amazon.com/dp/B00HKKCNNU

Miguel Cabrera

http://www.amazon.com/dp/B00HKG3G1W

Buster Posey

http://www.amazon.com/dp/B00KP11V9S

Lou Gehrig

http://www.amazon.com/dp/B00KOZMONW

Babe Ruth

http://www.amazon.com/dp/B00IS2YB48

Floyd Mayweather

http://www.amazon.com/dp/B00HLEX5O6

Anderson Silva

http://www.amazon.com/dp/B00HLBOVVU

Printed in Great Britain
by Amazon.co.uk, Ltd.,
Marston Gate.